SUSSEX MURDER STORIES

RECALLING THE EVENTS OF SOME OF SUSSEX'S
MOST WELL-KNOWN MURDERS

Neil Walden

BRADWELL
BOOKS

Published by Bradwell Books

9 Orgreave Close Sheffield S13 9NP

Email: books@bradwellbooks.co.uk

British Library Cataloguing in Publication Data: a catalogue record for this book is available from the British Library.

1st Edition

ISBN: 9781910551813

Print: Gomer Press, Llandysul, Ceredigion SA44 4JL

Artwork by: Andrew Caffrey

Photograph Credits: Photography by the Author
unless otherwise stated

ACKNOWLEDGEMENTS

I would particularly like to thank Croydon Museum for their help with providing local insight in the chapter dealing with the Greenhead case.

Thanks also to Bill Walden for providing the artist's impression of The Officer's House in The Crumbles, which was demolished many years ago.

CONTENTS

Arundel Castle
(iStock)

INTRODUCTION

The true murder stories to be found in this book come from both the east and west of the historic county of Sussex. The cases covered span the period from the middle of the nineteenth century to the middle of the twentieth century and all come from a time when the death penalty was still in place. There are sixteen murder cases related in these pages; nine of the murderers were sent to the scaffold, but several of the cases still remain unsolved.

While there are a couple of photographs of murderers, I have not used any pictures of crime scenes at the time of the murders themselves. In each case I have attempted to leave this to the imagination. Instead I have opted to show sites and scenes which are important to each case and that can still be seen today.

The title of each of the chapters is taken from the contemporary newspaper reports of the crimes. While several of the stories (that of John Haigh in particular) are fairly well known, there are other stories in this volume which have seldom been recounted since the time that the murder was committed. I hope you will find them of interest.

Neil Walden

THE CRUMBLES MURDER

ON 20 AUGUST 1920 A YOUNG BOY WALKING ON THE STRETCH OF BEACH KNOWN AS THE CRUMBLES, SITUATED BETWEEN EASTBOURNE AND PEVENSEY, STUMBLED ON SOMETHING PROTRUDING FROM THE SHINGLE. TO THE YOUNG BOY'S HORROR HE REALISED THAT IT WAS A HUMAN FOOT. THE POLICE WERE SUMMONED AND A BODY WAS RECOVERED. IT WAS FOUND TO BE A YOUNG WOMAN WHO HAD BEEN BLUDGEONED TO DEATH.

It wasn't long before witnesses came forward to confirm that they had seen two men and a girl walking near the railway tracks close to where the body was found. The three of them had been heading in the Pevensey direction and one of the men had his arm around the girl's waist. All three were said to be in high spirits.

Soon details of the tragic events were published in the local newspaper and the victim's landlady, from a nearby guesthouse, was alerted to what may have happened to her young guest who had failed to return the previous night. The landlady reported the missing girl and was taken to the mortuary where her worst fears were confirmed. She identified her guest and in particular was able to recognise the distinctive green coat which she had been wearing when she had first arrived.

The Beach at Pevensey looking towards The Crumbles (The Author)

The victim was named as 17-year-old Irene Munro and the full story could now be pieced together. While Irene was from London, she had been on holiday to Sussex before. The previous year she had visited Brighton; this time it was Eastbourne. With it being the height of the holiday season she had struggled at first to obtain a room. Finally she settled on the seaside guesthouse and with that organised she set about enjoying her holiday.

The next morning Irene had walked down to the beach across The Crumbles. A young naval stoker, William Putland, who was home on leave in Eastbourne, had been on the beach at that time. Putland became an important witness as he was convinced he had seen Irene both then and a couple more times afterwards. Once again it was her vivid green coat that had stuck in his mind.

Now the hunt was on for the two men who had been with Irene. The trail led to two young residents of Eastbourne, Jack Alfred Field and William Thomas Gray. On 24 August there was sufficient evidence for them to be arrested and interviewed by the police.

At twenty years of age Field was the younger of the two. He had been discharged from the Navy and had previously been in trouble with the law. An examination of his prison records show a spiralling succession of misdemeanours escalating from stealing a bicycle in Portsmouth to trespass and desertion. At the time of Irene's murder he claimed to be of no fixed abode but he was in fact staying at his parents' house in Susans Road, Eastbourne, close to the guesthouse where Irene had been staying.

The other suspect was aged 28 and was married. He gave his profession as a platelayer, a worker who maintained the railway track. However, the truth was that both Field and Gray were out of work and spent their time hanging around in town with little to do.

While further witnesses were now coming forward, both Field and Gray were telling roughly the same story. They claimed to have spent the day of Irene's death together, with a friend, at Pevensey Castle. Interestingly, however, the friend whom they both mentioned seemed to know nothing about this excursion. The two men were charged with the murder.

On 13 December 1920 the five-day trial began at the County Hall in Lewes. Inevitably the case for the prosecution had to be based on circumstantial evidence. No one had seen the crime committed and both the accused continued to plead not guilty. However, an impressive stream of witnesses were called to give evidence.

Field was the only witness called forward for his own defence but he was a particularly unsympathetic figure, behaving in a truculent way, keeping his hands thrust into his pockets and deliberately yawning. He denied much of the evidence already heard, but did at least now acknowledge that he and Gray had concocted the story about being in Pevensey with a friend.

In his summing-up, the judge said that there was no doubt that Irene Munro had been murdered. The joint charge meant that the men were acting together and it was immaterial which man had actually committed the violence. Dealing with the question of motive, the judge said it could either have been robbery or an attempt by the girl to resist an assault. The jury took an hour to return a guilty verdict for both men but with a recommendation for mercy on the grounds that they believed the crime was not premeditated.

Gray did not give evidence at the trial but he was more vocal at the appeal. In fact, part of his defence was that he had been committing a burglary at the critical time. It was an alibi that didn't elicit much sympathy. On top of this both Field and Gray claimed that the other had confessed to the crime. Of course these statements conflicted once more with their earlier accounts and the appeal was swiftly dismissed. The hangings of Field and Gray were carried out at Wandsworth Prison on 4 February 1921

A SHOOTING IN BOGNOR

IN FEBRUARY OF 1942 A YOUNG CANADIAN SOLDIER WHO WAS UNDER ARREST AT AN ARMY BARRACKS IN SUSSEX MANAGED TO ESCAPE INTO CENTRAL BOGNOR REGIS. HE BROKE INTO AN EMPTY HOTEL IN MARINE PARADE TO SPEND THE NIGHT AND TO STEAL CIVILIAN CLOTHES. THE NEXT DAY HE SLIPPED AWAY FROM THE CENTRE OF TOWN WITHOUT DETECTION. WITHIN A COUPLE OF DAYS HE WAS TO BECOME A DOUBLE MURDERER.

Over the next few days, after the escape from the barracks, several houses in Aldwick, just outside Bognor, were forcibly entered and property was stolen. Francis Joseph Fuller was the 56-year-old owner of a local market gardening business and he was also a Special Constable. He had been entrusted with looking after Nos 14 and 16, Fernhurst Gardens in Aldwick, which were currently unoccupied. On the morning of 26 February, Fuller visited the properties in his charge and on arrival discovered tht the windows of both houses had been forced.

Fuller suspected someone was actually still inside and so contacted Police Sergeant William Avis. Fuller met

Sergeant Avis nearby at 11.30am and both of them made their way into No. 16. Sergeant Avis led the way but as he crossed the hall he was confronted by a man holding a pistol. The gunman was Private John William David Moore from Chatham, Ontario, a soldier with the Canadian Highland Light Infantry.

Moore shot the sergeant in the chest. Francis Fuller immediately ran down the path away from the house and took cover behind the garden fence but, according to a witness account, Moore pursued and shot him. The gunman now returned to the hallway of the house where Sergeant Avis lay mortally wounded and fired a second shot at him. Avis was killed by the second shot to the head while Fuller was to die from his wound a few days later.

Rock Gardens Hotel where Moore initially hid (Creative Commons)

When news of the shootings broke, a plan was devised to throw a cordon around the district. A battalion of heavily armed troops joined the manhunt for Moore, who had slipped out of the empty house and was known to still be armed with his service revolver and ammunition. It was a tense few hours as there was every expectation that Moore would resist arrest. Cars were now stopped and all male passengers travelling on buses leaving the cordoned off area were asked to provide proof of their identity.

In fact Moore had already made his escape across fields to Bognor Station, where he waited for the London train. The booking clerk who issued the ticket for the 1.40pm Victoria train remembered the man well as he had paid his fare in shilling coins. The coins were the bulk of the money that Moore had scraped together after leaving a trail of broken gas meters in each of the places where he had been hiding for the past week. For now he had escaped capture.

That evening Moore checked into a hostel in Leicester Square where he spent the night before setting off again the following morning. Heading north, Moore attempted to see an aunt in Enfield but she was out at the time so he left her a note. The fugitive next turned up in South Mimms, on his way to Hatfield, which was about six or seven miles away.

Moore now stopped someone to ask directions in the latest leg of his escape plan but, unfortunately for him, the person he approached happened to be a sergeant in the Metropolitan Police. The sergeant asked for identification and, realising that he was now in trouble, Moore drew his gun and took the policeman hostage, making it clear that he had already killed two policemen and that he was happy to make it three.

Help was called to the scene and, using the cover of a passing lorry, the police were able to overcome Moore without any further shots being fired. Moore was taken to the local police station and then later conveyed to Police HQ at Chichester where he was charged with murder.

At the subsequent trial at the Old Bailey the doctors, called in for their expert opinions, pointed out that insanity was known to run in the Moore family. They also pointed out that the indifference he had shown to the victims of the crimes was equalled only by the indifference that he had showed towards his own future welfare. This passing interest in his own future seemed to extend to merely pointing out that he 'expected to get the hot seat'. That was never likely to happen, but the gallows was a real possibility.

On the second day of his trial, 23 April 1942, a verdict of 'Guilty but Insane' was returned and John Moore was ordered to be indefinitely detained at His Majesty's Pleasure.

THE DONKEY ROW MURDER

JOHN HOLLOWAY EXPLAINED HIS WIFE CELIA'S ABSENCE BY SAYING THAT SHE HAD LEFT BRIGHTON FOR LONDON AND WAS NOW WORKING AS A CHAMBERMAID FOR A FAMILY IN HOLBORN. HOWEVER, WITHIN A WEEK OF HER DISAPPEARANCE IN JULY 1831, HEAVY RAINS WERE ALREADY STARTING TO REOPEN A SHALLOW GRAVE IN PRESTON PARK.

John Holloway was born in Lewes in 1806. His father was a soldier and, when he was posted abroad, the young John was left in the care of his grandparents. Later, after his father was discharged from the forces, the whole Holloway family lived in Alfriston in East Sussex. John always had a dream of going to sea, and while this never materialised he did find some employment as a painter working on various ships based in Newhaven and Rye. Throughout this period it seems that Holloway was also involved in petty crime.

Celia Bashford met John Holloway at the Brighton Races. The two of them must have made quite a distinctive couple as John was no more than 5 feet 3 inches in height and yet he was said to tower over the even more diminutive Celia. The couple were to be together for about three years before Celia became pregnant. John had always been something of a womaniser and had no intention of marrying Celia. With no husband, she returned to her family home in Ardingly and applied to the parish for relief. John was named as the father and, as was common practice at this time, he was locked up in Lewes Prison until he agreed to marry Celia. After more than a month in prison John was released and the couple married in November 1826 and moved to Brighton. At this point in the story, despite his eventful life, John was still only twenty while Celia was ten years older.

Although the new baby did not survive long, for the time being the couple stayed together. John found employment working for the Naval Blockade Service, which was a precursor of the Coast Guard and was largely intended to counter smuggling. It was at this time that he met and fell in love with Ann Kennett.

When Ann became pregnant, John feared history would repeat itself and that he was facing another period in prison, so he duly married Ann in Rye in March 1830. As he had the drawback of having a wife already, John was obliged to use an alternative name. The wedding was conducted in the name of Goldsmith, which was John's mother's maiden name.

There followed a period of comparative prosperity

when John was able to make a comfortable living from his legitimate jobs supplemented with funds from the various scams that he was involved with. John's criminal activities usually involved circulating counterfeit coins and he would regularly move from town to town along the Sussex coast so that the crimes could not be attributed to him. Meanwhile, seeing that for once her estranged husband had a regular income, Celia decided to put in a request for some maintenance money. As a result Holloway was now ordered to pay Celia two shillings a week, which was more than half of his wages. Burning with resentment, Holloway now tried to think of a more permanent solution to his problems.

John visited Celia and suggested they should resume their relationship and that they should move into the new lodgings that he had obtained in North Steyne Row in Brighton, which was also known as Donkey Row. Celia was prepared to give their marriage one last chance, but this prospective new start was in fact to be the end for Celia. Soon after entering the new property Celia was strangled. Parts of Celia's body were hidden at John's former lodgings in Margaret Street. Then, in the dead of night, the rest of Celia's remains were put into a trunk and carried by wheelbarrow to Preston Park.

The Crown and Anchor in Preston Road occupying the site of the
original pub of that name where the inquest into Celia's death took place
(The Author)

Following the heavy rains, word spread about the grisly find in Preston Park and John quickly hurried home from his latest work, which was as a painter on the Chain Pier, and managed to get home to Ann. There followed a half-hearted attempt to leave Brighton but the game was up. Ann was duly arrested and Holloway quickly handed himself in.

The degree of Ann's involvement was always open to question. At times John would indicate that she was present in Donkey Row and complicit in the murder; at other times that she was wholly innocent. Whatever the truth of the matter, Ann Kennett was tried at Lewes Assizes in March 1832. To many people's surprise she was found not guilty of involvement in Celia's death. John, on the other hand, had already been found guilty of murder. He was executed at Horsham Gaol in December 1831.

MURDER ON THE BRIGHTON TRAIN

IT WAS LATE IN THE AFTERNOON OF JUNE 27 1881 WHEN 22-YEAR-OLD PERCY LEFROY MAPLETON STAGGERED OUT OF THE TRAIN AT PRESTON PARK STATION. HE WAS RUFFLED AND SPLATTERED WITH BLOOD AND WAS CLAIMING THAT HE HAD BEEN ATTACKED BY TWO MEN. OVER THE NEXT FEW HOURS IT EMERGED THAT IN FACT MAPLETON HIMSELF HAD COMMITTED A MURDER ON THE BRIGHTON TRAIN. BUT BY THE TIME THE TRUTH WAS KNOWN MAPLETON HAD DISAPPEARED.

Once a week 64-year-old Isaac Frederick Gold, a former stockbroker living in Clermont Terrace in Brighton, would travel to London to attend to his business. On that June afternoon in 1881 he was travelling on the 2.10pm train from London, expecting to arrive back at Preston Park by 3.30pm.

Soon to travel on the same train was Mapleton, who was a failed author, journalist and actor from

Carshalton in Surrey. By the time of the murder he was heavily in debt and on the verge of bankruptcy. Now, armed with a revolver, knife and what little money he had left, Mapleton travelled to London Bridge station and purchased a first-class single ticket to Brighton.

Mapleton left the train briefly at East Croydon and walked along the platform past the first-class section of the train until he spotted Mr Gold, who was sitting alone in a carriage. Mapleton sat opposite with every intention of committing a robbery as soon as he had the opportunity. To avoid witnesses and the possibility of anyone hearing a scuffle or gunshots, he decided to act once the train entered one of the tunnels on the route. In committing the robbery it seems that Mapleton fired three or four shots, but this was still insufficient to kill Mr Gold, who put up a ferocious fight for his life. Finally, in Balcombe Tunnel, which is two-thirds of the way to Brighton, Mapleton managed to open the carriage door and force the dead or dying Mr Gold out of the compartment and on to the track.

It turned out that Percy had not chosen the best victim. As well as the desperate struggle it now seemed that Mr Gold had very little money on him. What he had Percy took, along with Mr Gold's watch. Mapleton now had to get rid of as much evidence as possible. Percy threw his revolver, bloodstained collar and other incriminating evidence out of the window and concocted the story of having himself been the victim of an attack.

Despite the suspicious lack of any assailants and the shocking bloodstained appearance of the train carriage, at first everyone was sympathetic to Percy's plight. After providing statements and completing other formalities it was arranged for him to be accompanied back to London. Certainly there was concern for his injuries, but there was already some suspicion that everything was not quite as he had described it.

Soon two railway workers discovered Mr Gold's body in Balcombe Tunnel. The railwaymen quickly left the tunnel to report their find, but the news of the discovery did not reach Mapleton's entourage, now bound for London or, for that matter, Mr Gold's wife, who waited dutifully for the return of her husband at Preston Park station.

After giving his companions the slip, Percy attempted to cover his tracks further. He threw the stolen watch off Blackfriars Bridge and attempted to lay low. However, within 24 hours of Percy's escape, 'Wanted for Murder' police notices describing him began appearing all over London. Soon these were superseded by further posters, now offering a £200 reward for his arrest. Then, with Mapleton still proving elusive, The Daily Telegraph published an artist's impression of the fugitive. This was a new technique and while it created plenty of public interest it also resulted in alleged sightings of Mapleton all over the country.

It was now nearly a fortnight since the attack and throughout this time Percy had been hiding in Stepney under an assumed name. Now, desperately short of money, he broke cover and sent a telegram to his old employer asking for his wages to be sent to his lodgings at 32 Smith Street. The resulting knock on the door did not bring Mapleton the expected money; instead it was two police inspectors and he was placed under arrest.

THE BRIGHTON RAILWAY TRAGEDY — PERCY LEFROY MAPLETON BEFORE THE MAGISTRATES AT CUCKFIELD

Percy Lefroy Mapleton before the magistrates in Cuckfield
(The Graphic 23 July 1881 © Look and Learn)

On 4 November 4 1881 Mapleton stood trial before Lord Chief Justice Coleridge at the Maidstone Assizes. It took just ten minutes for the jury to decide that he was guilty.

While awaiting execution Mapleton made a series of statements providing a bewildering variety of confessions to Mr Gold's murder, each inventing different motives and methods. Eventually, having tired of his own case, he started confessing to other unsolved crimes, none of which could have contained any truth. Mapleton was hanged for the murder on the Brighton train in Lewes on 29 November 1881.

THE CUCKFIELD MYSTERY

ON 19 NOVEMBER 1869 EDWARD PECKHAM, WHO WAS A LABOURER AND RAT CATCHER IN CUCKFIELD, WAS ON HIS WAY TO WORK. AS HE PASSED THE REAR OF CUCKFIELD CHURCH HIS DOG BECAME INTERESTED IN SOMETHING IN A DITCH NEAR NEWBURY POND. IT WAS THE BODY OF A MURDERED MAN. THIS IS A CRIME THAT HAS YET TO BE SATISFACTORILY SOLVED.

After closer inspection it was thought that the dead man had been in the ditch for something like 24 hours. He was well dressed and 5 feet 6 inches in height with distinctive scars on the back of his neck and right wrist. The body was made available for inspection in the White Harte Inn in Cuckfield and over 200 people filed past in the hope that someone would recognise the stranger, but there was no success. The only clue to the identity of the dead man was a pawnbroker's ticket in his pocket made out in the name of John Williams.

The key to the Cuckfield mystery proved to be a robbery which had taken place in Croydon, 30 miles away, some months earlier. On 30 September 1869 the shop of Mr Harland, the jeweller, silversmith and clockmaker, situated at 11 North End was burgled and about £500 worth of jewellery was taken. There were few leads as to who had committed the burglary but eventually some rings, thought to originate from the crime, were bought by a tradesman.

Cuckfield Church, close to where the mysterious body was found
(The Author)

The tradesman in question was William Barclay of Battersea. In the middle of the night there was a police raid at the Barclay household and William was arrested. Barclay was charged with receiving gold rings knowing that they were stolen. On his arrest and throughout the trial he denied the charge, claiming that he had got the jewels in good faith from someone called James Greenhead. Certainly Barclay had been somewhat naive in trusting Greenhead and he even acknowledged that he had been warned not to have anything to do with him as he was a 'ticket-of-leave' man. This simply meant that he was a convict out on licence from prison.

While Barclay was acquitted of receiving the stolen property, some months later a bricklayer called Rowland was arrested for his involvement in the robbery as he was found to have a quantity of the stolen jewels. In his defence Rowland said that he had merely been storing them and that the culprit was, once again, James Greenhead. Throughout the two trials the real villain of the piece had seemingly disappeared, leaving a trail of misery in his wake.

We know little about Greenhead. What we do know is that on 31 May 1866 he had been released from Portsmouth prison after serving four years of a five-year sentence for burglary. Greenhead's prison records suggest that he was a model prisoner throughout his time at Millbank, Pentonville and finally Portsmouth prisons. Yet within months of release he was back up to his old tricks.

It was the superintendent of police for Hammersmith who first made the connection between the dead man found in Cuckfield and the Croydon burglary. He saw a photograph of Williams (as he was still thought to be at this time due to the pawnbroker's ticket) and identified him as the elusive James Greenhead.

Now it was thought that a crowbar that had been found near the Cuckfield murder victim, and possibly used to bludgeon him to death, was in fact the one used to break into the Croydon jewellers. The inquest into Greenhead's death now returned a verdict of 'wilful murder by some person or persons unknown'.

So just who did kill the robber James Greenhead? The main suspect has to be Rowland, who had been caught in possession of so much of the stolen property. Certainly his statements were full of inconsistencies which put him in the frame, but ultimately he was only ever to serve a year in prison, for his involvement in the robbery alone.

Another suspect could be the other receiver of stolen goods, William Barclay. However, the dramatic night-time raid and arrest at the Barclay household was purely because he and his brother John (who held down the responsible job of a teacher at the workhouse in Dudley) had made a visit to The Crystal Palace, a few miles away on Sydenham Hill, and had not been about earlier when the police had called. When the Barclays had got home they heard about the robbery and, putting two and two together, agreed that William would go to the police in the morning and explain that they thought they probably had some of the stolen items. Plenty were to testify to William's good character and it was a sequence of events verified by William's fiancé.

We now move on two years from the Cuckfield mystery. In September 1871, William Pettit and Hayton Waller were charged with being involved in the wilful murder of James Greenhead. The two men had been caught talking indiscreetly about the murder and the possible disposal of some rings that they now had in their possession. They seemed to be debating whether or not to hand the stolen goods in and attempt to claim a reward of £200 which had been offered at the time of the body's initial discovery.

The principal witness in the trial of these two suspects was James Edwards, landlord of the New Port tavern in Newhaven, who had witnessed the two men's conversation. Knowing that they had been overheard by the landlord it seems that the two suspects now claimed that they had seen the murder committed but were not responsible.

There was not enough evidence to convict Pettit and Waller and so they were able to walk free. With their release the trail went well and truly cold and the mystery of who murdered James Greenhead remains unsolved.

THE BRIGHTON MILITARY MURDER

ON 8 JUNE 1862 AN IRISH SOLDIER SERVING IN THE 18TH HUSSARS NAMED JOHN O'DEA ENTERED THE BARRACKS IN BRIGHTON FOR THE NIGHT. AS HE DID SO HE WAS CONFRONTED BY THE SENTRY ON DUTY. THE SENTRY CALLED FOR O'DEA TO IDENTIFY HIMSELF. NO SOONER HAD HE ANSWERED THAN THE GUARD RAISED HIS GUN AND SHOT HIM IN THE CHEST.

There was no hope for the 22-year-old O'Dea as the ball had passed right through him. The murderer offered little resistance to those coming to disarm him and he was immediately identified as a fellow Irishman and member of The Hussars, called John Flood. He was placed under arrest and handed over to the police.

The facts of the case as they emerged seemed straightforward. Flood was clearly responsible, a fact that he had never denied, and the two men had quarrelled, resulting in the murder of O'Dea. But as the inquest went on and the full story emerged there was some unease about returning a verdict that would send John Flood to the gallows.

John Flood was revealed to be a sober, well-behaved and quiet soldier. But he had been subjected to mock court-martials for petty misdemeanours by other members of the regiment. This totally unofficial process had turned Flood's life into a misery as he was regularly abused and whipped. The main protagonist in these mock trials had been O'Dea. The latest act of bullying had resulted in Flood being sent on 'stable duty', but supposedly he had left O'Dea's saddle dirty; Flood was therefore to be court-martialled once more and no doubt flogged. Determined that this should not happen again, Flood hid in the Guard Room and as O'Dea entered he shot him dead.

A witness at Flood's trial in Lewes in the summer of 1862, a sergeant, was to say that if he had known of these court martials he would have tried to stop them. He knew that the practice occurred in the army, but had not been aware that it was taking place in that regiment.

As the trial progressed there was a lot of bickering as to whether the accused was drunk or not. He had certainly had two glasses of rum, and the consensus of opinion was that he was partially intoxicated. One doctor at the scene of the incident had thought that Flood was behaving strangely and that he must have taken poison. In fact there was little chance of Flood poisoning himself as he was totally convinced of the justice of his actions.

The mitigating circumstances heard at the trial elicited nothing but sympathy in the press. The typical response was that if Flood was to go to the gallows then the result would be that there would be two murders rather than one. Yet he was still found guilty and duly sentenced to death. Far from appeals for clemency he was given the added stipulation that there was not the slightest hope of mercy. As Flood heard this he collapsed unconscious into the arms of his gaolers.

Flood was sent to Pentonville and thence to Portsmouth to await his execution. In the end, with some ten days left to the date of his hanging, the Home Secretary decided on a reprieve and the death penalty was commuted to penal servitude for life. In most people's eyes this punishment was more fitting for the crime that Flood had committed.

Little more was now heard of John Flood. Three years later he was transported, along with nearly 300 other convicts, to Western Australia where he was to end his days.

THE CASE OF THE SOLDIER CLEARY

ANOTHER MILITARY MURDER, PLAYING OUT AT ABOUT THE SAME TIME AS THE SHOOTING OF JOHN O'DEA, TOOK PLACE IN THE SOMERSTOWN AREA OF CHICHESTER. A POLICEMAN WAS ON DUTY JUST BEFORE MIDNIGHT ON 16 OCTOBER 1861 AND HEARD SHOUTING AND THE SOUND OF GUNFIRE. THE POLICEMAN HURRIED TO THE NEARBY BARRACKS AND THEN WITH THREE SOLDIERS HE WENT TO INVESTIGATE WHAT HAD HAPPENED. IN THE FIELDS AROUND BISHOP OTTER COLLEGE THEY FOUND A STUDENT WHO HAD BEEN SHOT AND MORTALLY WOUNDED.

The student was James Outen, who was 22 years of age. He was local to the area having been brought up on the Stansted Park estate, not far from Chichester, where his father worked as a blacksmith. That night Outen had been returning from the city centre where he had been to visit a friend in St John's Street. At the time he was found he was still fully conscious and was able to confirm that he had been shot by a man who had been sitting on a gate, and that the man had been a soldier. The young student was taken back inside the college where despite all efforts to save him he died.

In no time a story was circulated that the fatal bullet was fired by a soldier from the 59th Foot Regiment (Company 12) and that he had been intending to kill his major, a much despised officer named Bush, who had in fact passed up the road some ten minutes earlier on his way to his quarters.

The most likely candidate for the assassin was found to be a soldier called Cleary who was from Nenagh, County Tipperary, Ireland. At this point he was still missing, along with a rifle and ammunition.

The day after the shooting the barracks supplied 200 men to help in the search for Cleary. While he initially proved to be elusive the rifle and ammunition were quickly found in the nearby water meadows close to the White Swan pub and not far from the scene of the shooting.

The manhunt came to an end at Coultershaw Bridge, well on the way towards Petworth and about 15 miles from the city centre. Here Cleary was apprehended by two policemen who saw him in the road. Cleary looked pretty conspicuous due to the uniform that he was still wearing, and although he attempted a half-hearted escape by jumping over a hedge and into a field of turnips, he was soon caught and placed firmly under arrest and taken back to Chichester.

With Cleary under arrest the full story began to unfold. It seems that on the night of the shooting he had been ordered to do extra drill. And at this point he must have decided to desert. Cleary left the dormitory on the pretext of feeling unwell. That much was pretty much agreed by everyone. However, Cleary claimed to be totally innocent of the shooting, saying that he had been in Littlehampton at the time of the murder.

Perhaps the case was not as clear cut as initially assumed. No one could swear that Cleary had his rifle with him. It could conceivably be that he was being framed, with another soldier taking the rifle in the hope of shooting Major Bush and deflecting the blame onto the recently deserted Cleary.

It is difficult to believe that Major Bush had inspired such murderous hatred amongst his own men but there is certainly evidence to that effect. Indeed, there is even evidence that he was shot at by his own men during the time that the regiment was posted to China.

At Cleary's trial the testimonies from a whole succession of witnesses who had either seen or heard the incident were far from conclusive. Other than saying that the man who pulled the trigger was a soldier, no one could definitely identify Cleary. In fact there were sightings of other soldiers in the vicinity of the shooting on the evening in question.

If the intended target had been the hated Major Bush then, regardless of who pulled the trigger, something very serious must have gone wrong. It was a bright night and Outen, the young student, bore no resemblance to the major. However, Cleary's defence did not suggest that it was a case of mistaken identity, as their case was that Cleary was wholly innocent.

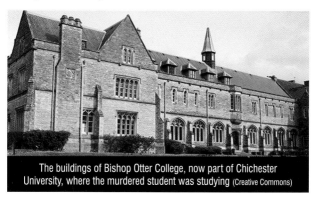

The buildings of Bishop Otter College, now part of Chichester University, where the murdered student was studying (Creative Commons)

There was certainly an element of doubt in the jury's mind and they delivered a verdict of not guilty. However, Cleary's ordeal was to continue as he was soon to be court-martialled for the military offence of desertion. He was duly found guilty of this lesser offence and served a sentence of four years' penal servitude at Millbank Prison.

THE BRIGHTON POISONING CASE

IT WAS IN THE EARLY 1870s THAT CHRISTIANA EDMUNDS CONDUCTED HER POISONING CAMPAIGN. SHE ATTEMPTED TO POISON HER LOVER'S WIFE AND SEVERAL OTHER PEOPLE IN BRIGHTON BEFORE ADOPTING A MORE RANDOM APPROACH. SHE OBTAINED CHOCOLATE CREAMS AND, AFTER LACING THEM WITH STRYCHNINE, WOULD RETURN THEM TO THE SHOP FROM WHERE THEY HAD BEEN BOUGHT. THE SHOPKEEPER, NOT KNOWING THEM TO BE POISONED, WOULD THEN SELL THEM A SECOND TIME. IT WAS BY THIS MEANS THAT CHRISTIANA WAS TO MURDER SIDNEY BARKER.

Christiana Edmunds was born in Margate in 1828. She lived for some years in Canterbury. But it was after moving to Gloucester Place in Brighton, with her widowed mother, that she met and became infatuated by Dr Charles Beard, who lived at 64 Grand Parade with his wife Emily and their children.

When Charles had attempted to end their relationship, Christiana had visited the Beards' house with a gift of chocolates for Emily. The following day Mrs Beard became violently ill, but fortunately recovered. Dr Beard had his suspicions that she had been poisoned but he was desperate to keep his relationship with Christiana secret and so did not report the incident.

Edmunds carried on with her activities unabated. Using the alias of Miss Wood from Kingston in Surrey, she was obtaining the strychnine from a chemist called Dr Isaac Garrett, who was based in The Queen's Road. This was done on the pretence that she needed it to poison cats that had been making a mess in her garden. This was not the greatest cover story as Dr Garrett didn't like the sound of his strychnine being used in that way and told her that she would have to get her poison elsewhere. Next time Christiana visited Garrett she changed her story and said that she was in fact going to poison a dog. Now banned from the chemist on the grounds of cruelty, Christiana managed to get her supply of strychnine from a dressmaker friend called Caroline Stone who acted on her behalf.

Soon she was using another emissary, a boy named Adam May, to purchase the chocolates on her behalf since she was starting to draw too much attention to herself with her constant purchases. May simply believed that he was running an innocent errand for Christiana.

While several people in Brighton had become ill, no one had connected the illnesses with the chocolates. That was until June 1871 when the Barker family came on a day trip to Brighton. Uncle Charles visited Maynards, the confectioners, thinking that some sweets would be a nice present for four-year-old Sidney. Several members of the family ate a chocolate and found the distinctive metallic flavour to not be to their taste and spat them out. Unfortunately Sidney did not do the same.

A verdict of 'accidental death' was recorded by the coroner. Maynards disposed of all existing stock and was then allowed to resume trading. Also conducting business as usual was Christiana.

Dr Beard, still estranged from Christiana, was watching from afar and finally could not keep quiet any longer. Following his statement, the police came to interview Christiana. They were to find her reclining on a couch at her mother's house, supposedly too feeble to stand after eating a poisoned apricot from a basket of fruit sent to her by a deranged poisoner. The police were not fooled and she was soon charged with the attempted murder of Emily Beard.

At Christiana's trial at the Old Bailey in January 1872, her mother testified that both sides of their family had a history of mental illness. Dr Beard was to claim that he and Edmunds never had a proper relationship, but that instead it was merely a series of flirtatious letters sent by her to him. The defence, however, was able to indicate that the two had in fact become involved in an affair, arguing that it was this that had sent Edmunds over the edge into madness.

It took the jury only an hour to deliver their verdict. Then there was a further hour needed to disprove Christiana's dramatic assertion that she was pregnant. At last the judge sentenced Christiana to death, but this was then commuted to life imprisonment due to her mental state.

Looking across the gardens from Gloucester Place. Dr Beard's house would be under what is now the University buildings
(Mike Quinn)

After the trial things returned to normal in Brighton. Dr Beard and his family remained in Brighton and by the 1890s they were living in German Place, which is now Madeira Place, just off the seafront. Meanwhile Christiana was to spend the rest of her days in Broadmoor, where she was to die in 1907.

A SECOND CRUMBLES MURDER

AFTER A DAY SPENT IN EASTBOURNE, ETHEL DUNCAN AND HER NEW BOYFRIEND TOOK A TAXI THE THREE MILES TO HIS SEASIDE BUNGALOW IN THE CRUMBLES. AS SOON AS SHE ENTERED, IT WAS FAIRLY OBVIOUS EVEN TO THE INFATUATED ETHEL THAT ANOTHER WOMAN HAD BEEN THERE. ETHEL WAS ALSO TO OBSERVE A LARGE BROWN TRUNK IN ONE OF THE BEDROOMS, BUT UNBEKNOWNST TO HER THIS STILL CONTAINED THE BODY OF HIS PREVIOUS GIRLFRIEND.

Miss Emily Beilby Kaye was from Prestwich in Lancashire. She had been born in 1885 and was known to have been careful with her money. Her working life started in her parents' confectionery shop in Chorlton, but soon she was working as a typist in Manchester and sharing her lodgings with her sister.

Herbert Mahon was born in Liverpool in 1889. By the age of 21 he was married but still living with his parents in West Derby and working as a clerk. Soon he was to become involved in a series of offences involving embezzlement and deceiving young women. Eventually he received a term of five years in prison for assaulting a young woman with a hammer after she had interrupted him while breaking into the National Provincial Bank. After his release from prison Pat Mahon, as he was now known, worked as a soda-fountain salesman in southern England. It was here that he met Emily, who was now living and working in London.

Mahon started a relationship with Emily and they spent some time together in Hampshire. Emily seemed besotted, and rather indiscreetly boasted that she was engaged to the still married Mahon and that, subsequent to the wedding, they were going to emigrate to South Africa. It seems that Emily believed that Mahon had managed to obtain lucrative employment in Cape Town.

Matters reached a head in April 1924. On 7 April Emily left for Eastbourne, where Mahon had rented The Officer's House on The Crumbles for three months. The house had obtained its name from once being the home of the officer in charge of the coastguard station. Whatever Mahon's plans were at this juncture there was an added complication. He had now met Ethel Duncan.

On Good Friday in 1924, Mahon met Ethel at Eastbourne Station. Mahon explained away the items of women's clothing in the house and eventually screwed the door shut on the room containing the suspicious-looking trunk. The two of them then settled down to enjoy their long weekend at The Officer's House.

Easter Saturday saw Ethel going shopping while Mahon attended the racing at the nearby track in Plumpton, although not before he sent himself a telegram fabricating an urgent meeting which would cut short their weekend. The following day they took the 3.30pm train back to London and, that evening, they dined together before finally going to a show in the West End called The Whirl of The World. Before long it would be Ethel's world that was in a whirl as she was to be called as a witness in a celebrated murder trial.

Throughout this entire period Mahon had been married, and it was at this point that his wife's patience finally snapped. She now suspected that her husband was up to his old tricks again. Finding a left luggage ticket in one of his suit pockets, she sent a trustworthy friend, an ex-policeman, to Waterloo Station to redeem the luggage. The contents of the bag included bloodstained clothing and a knife. With the bag and ticket returned to their original places, a police watch was placed on the cloakroom. They didn't have to wait long as the following day Mahon came to collect the bag.

Royal Hotel Eastbourne where Mahon and Ethel dined on the evening
of Good Friday 1924 (Creative Commons)

Now under arrest, Mahon claimed that he had been using the bag to carry home meat to feed the dogs. The unlikely story might have accounted for the bloodstained clothing but not the accompanying knife. Even this story was quickly abandoned as he realised the situation was hopeless as the blood and clothing were clearly Emily's and her body would soon be discovered.

The Officers House at the time of the murder. It is long-demolished to prevent sightseers (Bill Walden)

Mahon's later statements recounted how he and Emily had quarrelled and that she had turned violent and attempted to attack him with an axe that was used for cutting the coal. In the commotion she had fallen and struck her head on the coal scuttle and promptly died.

45

A search of The Officer's House showed no sign of an axe attack or any battle with the fire irons, but there were parts of Emily's body and a great mass of forensic evidence; not least the totally undamaged and rather fragile-looking coal scuttle that clearly had not been the cause of death.

Mahon was charged with Emily's murder and his trial began on 15 July 1924 at Sussex Assizes in Lewes. The most damning evidence, which seemed to fly in the face of an accidental death, was the premeditated nature of the attack, borne out by the fact that Mahon had bought the knife used in the murder shortly in advance of Emily's death.

Much of the trial hinged around establishing a motive for the murder. Perhaps it was because she was pregnant? But just as likely was the fact that Mahon had no further use for Emily. While she was comparatively well off at the time that they first met, her money had now dwindled as Mahon had extorted most of it from her.

Mahon was found guilty and sentenced to death. The execution took place at Wandsworth Prison on 3rd September 1924.

THE ACID BATH MURDERS

JOHN HAIGH WAS ONE OF THE MOST NOTORIOUS KILLERS IN BRITISH HISTORY. OFFICIALLY HE MURDERED SIX PEOPLE, BUT WE CAN NEVER BE CERTAIN AS TO THE ACTUAL NUMBER AS THE BODIES WERE NEVER FOUND, EACH OF THEM HAVING BEEN DISSOLVED IN SULPHURIC ACID.

Haigh was born in Stamford in 1909 and had a very religious upbringing in Yorkshire. He was responsible for some minor thefts, which escalated into more substantial frauds. In November 1934 he received a 15-month sentence in Wakefield Prison.

When released from prison Haigh became a chauffeur to William McSwan, a wealthy man who owned a number of amusement arcades. Although he appeared to have given up his life of crime throughout this period, he was in fact supplementing his pay with further fraudulent activities. Haigh even pretended to be a solicitor operating out of three offices, one of which he claimed was in Hastings. This time, when he was caught, Haigh was to receive a four-year prison sentence.

While in Lincoln Prison Haigh worked in the tinsmith's

shop and so would have come into contact with acid. Seeing its destructive power, it is said that he started to concoct what he thought would be the perfect murder. It would be a crime where the body would never be found, largely because it would have been completely dissolved in sulphuric acid.

Whenever he was out of prison Haigh never seemed to struggle to find employment and by 1943 he was an accountant with an engineering firm. Soon after, by chance, he again bumped into William McSwan. His former employer introduced Haigh to his parents, who mentioned that they had invested their money in property.

On 6 September 1944, William McSwan disappeared. In reality Haigh had murdered him, but he told the parents that their son had gone into hiding to avoid being called up for the army. Haigh then took over McSwan's house and assets, making sure that letters arrived, supposedly from the dead man, who he pretended was hiding in Scotland, to put his parents' minds at rest. When the Second World War came to an end they became curious as to why their son had not returned. Haigh's response to this was to murder them too.

Between 1945 and 1947 Haigh swindled more than £6,000 from the McSwan estate and, on the strength of it, moved into a London hotel. However, before long he had gambled away the McSwans' money and was on the lookout for another couple to kill and rob. He settled upon a Dr Archibald Henderson and his wife, Rose.

Haigh now moved to Sussex. He rented a small workshop at 2 Leopold Road in Crawley. On 12 February 1948, Haigh drove the recently befriended Henderson to Crawley from the Metropole Hotel in Brighton, on the pretext of showing him an invention of his. When they arrived Haigh shot Henderson in the head with a revolver that he had earlier stolen from the doctor's own house. He then lured Mrs Henderson to the workshop, claiming her husband had fallen ill, and shot her also.

After disposing of the Hendersons' bodies in oil drums filled with acid, he forged a letter from them putting himself in charge of their affairs. He now set about selling their property and belongings. Nearly £8,000 was taken from the estate of the Hendersons, who had supposedly emigrated to South Africa. Yet within six months Haigh was short of money once again.

Haigh's final victim was Olive Durand-Deacon, who he had met at the hotel in London. She was interested in the inventions that Haigh claimed that he had made and she was lured to the Crawley workshop where she was duly murdered. Two days later Durand-Deacon's friend, Constance Lane, reported her missing. Constance had bumped into Olive on the steps of the hotel and she had told her that she was just off to Crawley with Mr Haigh.

The Metropole hotel in Brighton where Haigh entertained
The Hendersons on the night before their murder (Creative Commons)

Detectives soon discovered Haigh's record of theft and fraud and searched the workshop. Police not only found Haigh's attaché case containing a dry cleaner's receipt for Mrs Durand-Deacon's coat, but also papers referring to the Hendersons and McSwans. There was also all of Haigh's paraphernalia relating to the acid, although the full significance of that was probably not realised at first.

A Horsham jeweller now reported that he had been sold jewellery matching the description of the items worn by Olive when she had disappeared. The seller was supposedly a Mr McLean, but he clearly matched the description of Haigh. Soon forensic evidence revealed that the bodies had been dissolved in acid.

John George Haigh taken at Horsham Police station 1949
(Creative Commons)

Things looked pretty bleak for Haigh. After his arrest he pleaded insanity, but the premeditated nature of the crimes and the fact that he had previously asked about Broadmoor, and his chances of ever gaining a release from such an establishment, counted against him.

Haigh confessed to the six murders and also to three others, including a Welsh girl called Mary, who he claimed to have bumped into in Eastbourne. While the police did not believe this confession, it cannot be entirely discounted. Less credible was the notion that he was in fact a blood-drinking vampire. Surely this story was invented by Haigh in an attempt to prove his insanity.

The trial took place at Lewes Assizes in July 1949 over a two-day period. It took only seventeen minutes for the verdict of guilty to be returned. Haigh was sentenced to death and was executed at Wandsworth Prison on 10 August 1949.

THE CROWBOROUGH TRAGEDY

IN 1922, NORMAN THORNE, USING MONEY LOANED TO HIM BY HIS FATHER, MOVED TO CROWBOROUGH TO SET UP A CHICKEN FARM. HE WAS REGULARLY VISITED BY HIS FIANCÉ, ELSIE, AND ALL SEEMED TO BE GOING WELL UNTIL HE MET AND FELL IN LOVE WITH A LOCAL GIRL.

Norman had been born in Portsmouth in 1901. His father was a steam engine manufacturer at the docks. Later the family moved to Kensal Green in London and Norman started work at an engineering company. By 1917 Norman was also a Sunday School teacher and had met up with Elsie Cameron, a typist working at a glassworks, who attended the same church. They were to become romantically involved.

The situation became difficult when Elsie was no longer able to work due to her poor nerves. This was exacerbated by Norman losing his own job. With money now tight, Norman moved to Crowborough and started to set up his new business, the Wesley Poultry Farm. Norman's plan was that he would live alone on the site, looking after the poultry and trying to build up the business. Elsie would visit whenever she could, although the conditions were so primitive that she would always lodge elsewhere in the town.

Living a lonely life away from his family, it was almost inevitable that Norman would meet someone else. Attending a dance he became acquainted with Elizabeth Ann Coldicott, who was known as Bessie. Norman's new girlfriend was a Brighton-born dressmaker and, unlike Elsie, lived full-time in Crowborough. In fact her house, over towards the Beacon golf course, was just a stone's throw from the home of Sir Arthur Conan Doyle. Undeterred by the close proximity of Sherlock Holmes's creator, Norman hatched a plan to get out of his difficult situation.

By this time Elsie was pressing for marriage, telling Norman that she was pregnant. Norman remained infatuated with Bessie and was determined to break off the engagement. However, he felt that, in view of her bad nerves, it would be kinder to bide his time and do it gently.

In November 1924 there was an exchange of letters between Norman and Elsie. Norman tried to explain the situation, but Elsie seemed not to understand and so Norman became blunter in his approach. When the penny finally dropped the reply from Elsie wasn't exactly what Norman had hoped for:

'You have absolutely broken my heart, I never thought you were capable of such deception … Your duty is to marry me. I have first claim on you. I expect you to marry me as soon as possible.'

On 30 November Elsie turned up in Crowborough to further press her case, but Norman had no intention of ceasing his relationship with Bessie. Still not taking no for an answer, Elsie set off for Sussex once again on 5 December 1924. This was to be her last journey.

Days passed with no news from Elsie and her family grew increasingly concerned. Norman claimed not to know anything, and his ignorance of her whereabouts seemed to be borne out by the letters he was still sending to her saying that he had waited at Groombridge Station for her and that she had not turned up.

The police became involved when two nurserymen came forward and said they had been passing by Norman's gate and had seen Elsie walking in the direction of the farm on the evening of 5 December. At this point the police searched the huts on the farm but found no trace of Elsie. All the time Norman insisted she had never been there.

In early January 1925, a woman came forward to tell the police that she had been on her way home on the evening of 5 December when she had seen a young woman actually entering Thorne's farm. It wasn't much to go on, but the police now had three witnesses saying they had seen Elsie near or actually at the farm on the night in question. Chief Inspector Gillan of Scotland Yard now arrived at the poultry farm and Thorne was taken into custody.

Groombridge station, now part of The Spa Valley Railway, where Thorne claimed to have waited for Elsie
(Mark Hemsley)

A more through police search now located what was clearly Elsie's suitcase, containing her glasses, jumper and shoes, buried at the farm. Back at the police station, Norman could see that his original story would not hold water and so he gave another statement. He now claimed that Elsie had indeed called on him on the afternoon of 5 December. They had a raging argument and then he had gone out. While he was out Elsie hanged herself in frustration. If the police were surprised by this account of events, then the subsequent admission must have left them astounded: Norman now said that he realised that he would be implicated in the murder and that, under the circumstances, it was probably best to dismember and bury the body. The police were not impressed by the explanation and, with Elsie's remains having now been found buried on the farm, Norman Thorne was duly charged with her murder.

The trial took place at the Lewes Assize Court. Norman's defence remained true to his original explanation that this was suicide not murder and a picture was painted of Elsie as someone who was often depressed or hysterical. However, the prosecution pointed to the results of experiments carried out on the beam from which Elsie was said to have been hanged. There were no marks left to show where a rope had been fastened. In fact Elsie's injuries were more consistent with having received a heavy blow to the head rather than a hanging.

There was to be just one hanging in the Crowborough tragedy. That was to be of Norman Thorne, who was sentenced to death and executed at Wandsworth Prison on 22 April 1925.

THE BRIGHTON TRUNK MURDER

ON 15 JULY 1934 THE POLICE DISCOVERED THE BODY OF VIOLET SAUNDERS IN A TRUNK IN KEMP STREET IN BRIGHTON. ALMOST SIMULTANEOUSLY PARTS OF ANOTHER BODY HAD BEEN FOUND IN A TRUNK AT THE LEFT LUGGAGE OFFICE AT BRIGHTON STATION. ALTHOUGH THE FIRST MURDER WAS UNRELATED TO THE SECOND, IT DID LEAD TO AN ENORMOUS INTEREST IN THESE TWIN TRUNK MURDERS. ONLY ONE OF THEM WAS EVER SOLVED AND EVEN THEN THE MURDERER WALKED FREE.

Violet Saunders was the married name of Violet Watts, although she frequently preferred to be known as Violet Kaye. She was a former music-hall dancer and by 1934 she was living with a younger man who was also known to enjoy a rich variety of aliases. By this time he was generally known as Tony Mancini. Mancini was in his mid-twenties and was a petty criminal and one-time fairground boxer who in the past had worked with London gangsters. He was now living in Brighton and working in various capacities at an establishment called the Skylark Café.

One-time location of the Skylark Café, on the seafront between the two Brighton piers (The Author)

The relationship between Mancini and Violet was a tempestuous one. She was not above turning up at the café and causing a scene, usually based on her belief that Mancini was showing too much interest in the other waitresses. After one such incident Violet mysteriously disappeared. When asked, Mancini explained that she had taken a job in France and would be working in Montmartre for two years. He even produced a telegram, supposedly from Violet, supporting this story.

Largely due to the police interest in the other trunk murder, Violet's absence was noted and Mancini was questioned. Realising that the 'gone to France' alibi was unlikely to hold water, Mancini panicked and went on the run.

The police soon received a tip-off from a decorator working at a house in Brighton that something strange was going on. Investigating further, they stumbled on Violet's remains. The house was not where Mancini and Violet had been living together, but rather Violet's body, inside a trunk, had moved house with him. The trunk, now at the foot of the bed, was being used as a coffee table.

With Mancini having disappeared, a manhunt ensued. In fact he had gone to London to hide out with the criminal gangs that he had once worked with. They

weren't pleased to see him and he moved on again, soon spending his time in a hostel, trying to fabricate a better alibi. Eventually he was located in the Blackheath area of South London and placed in police custody.

Left Luggage office at Brighton station. Now a bar
(The Author)

Mancini's story was that he had seen Violet at the

Skylark and that she was drunk. When he came home later he found her dead. It didn't sound a terribly compelling defence and failed to explain why he had not gone to the police. Mancini's answer to that was that as he was well known to them he didn't believe that he would get a fair hearing. It was a theory that was soon to be tested.

Mancini's trial began at Lewes Assizes on 10 December 1934. The prosecution focused on Violet's death by a blow to the head. One witness said that Mancini had asked her to provide a false alibi. A graphologist later confirmed that the handwriting on the form for the phoney telegram matched Mancini's.

The police had recovered the charred remains of a hammer from the basement of Mancini's flat. However, the defence pointed out that there was no blood on the hammer and that blood found on Mancini's clothes may not have been as conclusive as first believed. One of the items of clothing was new and had not been purchased until after Violet was already dead. A number of witnesses also confirmed that Mancini and Kaye had seemed a contented couple. Perhaps Violet's death really was an accident, with her having fallen down the steps into the flat.

The unfolding story of this murder as well as the other trunk murder captured the interest of the nation, with news of the two literally running in parallel on the front pages of the newspapers, where they were referred to as

Trunk Mystery One and Trunk Mystery Two. The police had confirmed that the two cases were not connected but the connection seemed to stick. That Mancini was clearly not responsible for one case seemed to suggest in some way that he may not have been responsible for the second case, and after two and a quarter hours of deliberations the jury returned a verdict of not guilty.

It seems that Mancini expected to be convicted and he was at something of a loose end when that did not happen. He was soon touring fairgrounds once again, this time trading on his notoriety. Then, once the case was no longer in the public eye, he spent time overseas before settling in the North of England.

In 1976 Mancini told The News of the World that he had got away with murder and related what he said were

Tony Mancini as he was in 1934
(Creative Commons)

the true events of that day forty years earlier when he now admitted that he had killed Violet with the hammer. This is probably as near to the truth as we will get. By the end of his life, with the money from the newspaper exclusive long spent, Mancini was once again claiming he was innocent.

MURDER AT HASTINGS GAOL

IT WAS JUST AFTER SEVEN O'CLOCK IN THE MORNING ON MONDAY 10 MARCH 1856 WHEN JAMES WELLERD, THE KEEPER OF THE BOROUGH PRISON IN HASTINGS, WAS MURDERED BY A PRISONER.

Moments after the attack, passers-by were able to hear screams for help coming from the gaol itself, along with further calls coming from the windows of The King's Head Inn, which was situated directly opposite the gaol in Bourne Street. The cries from the pub had been from the landlord, Mr Pace, who was calling for assistance having just witnessed a daring escape.

Members of the public now attempted to get into the gaol. where the gaoler was lying on the ground and clearly in a bad way. The door to the gaol was finally opened by Mrs Ann Wellerd, who was married to the son of the injured man, and had been the one calling for help from inside the gaol.

Mrs Wellerd's account of the incident was that overnight there had been two pickpockets on remand at the gaol. The one who had made the escape was John Murdock, who was a seasoned criminal in his early twenties. The second pickpocket was a boy of just twelve, named George Wright. When they had been briefly released from the cell Murdock had attacked the elderly gaoler in the kitchen. Murdock had Wellerd in an arm-lock around the throat. He obviously exercised considerable force as it was sufficient to kill the older man.

The criminals sought unsuccessfully to find the keys to the front door. They were soon aware of Mrs Wellerd's screams from nearby and Murdock grabbed a poker from beside the fire and started issuing threats. Then he turned his attention to making his escape and from the back yard he managed to get on to the top of the perimeter wall via the roof of the coal shed. He briefly attempted to pull his fellow prisoner up after him but failed. Now in full view of the landlord of the pub opposite Murdock dropped down into the street below and quickly made his escape. Wright, the other criminal, was stranded in the yard and, now aware of the severity of the crime that he was involved in, fully cooperated with the authorities. A doctor was called but it was found to be too late to help the stricken gaoler.

Inspector Battersby of the local police arrived and set off in pursuit of Murdock, who had last been seen hurrying along All Saints' Street. But for the moment he evaded capture.

With the trail cold, Battersby sent word to all the nearby police stations and formed a cordon around the town in the hope of heading off any chance of escape.

Seven hours after the escape, a young child was playing in a field near the castle when she spotted someone lurking in a ditch beneath a hedge. She was aware of the manhunt and attracted the attention of some young lads, and they went to investigate. Murdock threatened the boys and told them not to follow him as he made his escape. He now headed west with the boys following at a safe distance. Others joined the pursuit and Murdock gathered speed. His clothes were already badly torn from the spikes on the gaol wall and he now threw his boots away to enable him to move more freely. In the region of the Priory Meadow (where the shopping centre of that name is now situated) Murdock was cornered. Two labourers detained him in Russell Street and soon after an arrest was made.

Back at the police station Murdock sought confirmation that Wellerd was dead, and on hearing that he was, he realised that he was in real trouble and spent the afternoon reading the Bible and threatening to kill himself in equal measure. Murdock made a point of saying how kindly the gaoler had been and how well he had been treated. He particularly asked that his mother might come and see him at his trial as he feared that he would never see her again if she did not.

Certainly Murdock was not optimistic about his own prospects, although the future of Wright was more in the balance as it rather depended on the level of premeditation. There had been talk from a previous occupant of the gaol, of having heard Murdock and Wright talking about throwing pepper into the face of Ann Wellerd should she intervene in the escape, but in the end George Wright was spared the gallows.

Largely as a consequence of the escape, the gaol was closed and the building later became a police station. By the middle of the twentieth century Bourne Street had completely disappeared under a new road that was built to ease congestion within the old town. By this time Lewes Prison had long been used to house local prisoners, and it was at Lewes Prison that Murdock was executed on 5 August 1856, an event witnessed by some 2,000 people.

Rock-A-Nore Rd looking up All Saints' Street where the prisoner made his escape
(N Chadwick)

THE ARUNDEL MURDER

JOAN WOODHOUSE WAS A 27-YEAR-OLD LIBRARIAN LIVING IN LONDON. IN AUGUST 1948 SHE WROTE TO HER FATHER, WHO LIVED IN YORKSHIRE, TO SAY THAT SHE WOULD BE VISITING HIM SHORTLY. IT SEEMS THAT SHE MUST HAVE HAD A CHANGE OF HEART AND THAT INSTEAD SHE SET OFF FOR SUSSEX. A FEW DAYS LATER HER BODY WAS DISCOVERED IN THE GROUNDS OF ARUNDEL PARK. SHE HAD BEEN STRANGLED.

What we do know is that Joan caught the train to Worthing and then a bus to Arundel. She was certainly in the busy square in Arundel in the early afternoon before walking up to Arundel Castle and into Arundel Park. Once there she found a remote part of the park to sunbathe. At some point that afternoon she was attacked and murdered. It was ten days before her strangled body was found by a local man, 24-year-old Thomas Stillwell, who had been working as a painter.

The initial viewpoint of the police was that Joan must have visited Worthing in order to meet up with a man and that the assailant was probably an acquaintance of hers. In fact Joan's diary contained the contact details of about 100 possible men as she was the secretary of an association linking librarians throughout Britain.

Precious time seemed to slip away as the police interviewed any men thought to be in the area who were of the correct sort of age to have known Joan. Initially they were throwing resources at finding witnesses of Joan's arrival in Arundel in the belief that the murderer was known to her and travelled down from London with her. As time went on, and with few leads coming to light, it now seemed more possible that maybe this was simply an opportunistic crime. Attention began to turn on to Stillwell, the man who discovered the body. Stillwell lived in a cottage in nearby Offham and had been seen in the park on the day of the murder.

Stillwell was interviewed on a number of occasions, although the results were ambiguous. Some of the time it seemed as if he had seen or even spoken to Joan. Other times he was far less certain about his facts and it was unclear if he had encountered her at all. His main alibi was that he was in Littlehampton, shopping and going to the cinema, followed by an evening in the pub playing darts.

The basis of one theory was that Stillwell had killed Joan but, not hearing anything about the body being found, he became curious as to whether it was still in the park. He had then returned to the scene of the crime and ended up reporting the discovery of the body himself. But other than this theory, the trail seemed to have gone cold.

With the initial failure of the police to find the culprit, Joan's family, armed with a reward that was being offered by The News of the World and their own private detective, set off for Arundel. The family's detective was Thomas Jacks and he was an interesting character. He was a former East Riding detective-sergeant turned private eye. By this time he was the proprietor of a Bridlington-based detective agency.

Jacks was not exactly working undercover and he appeared to enjoy the newspaper coverage. Soon he was happily giving quotes to the various newspapers on his way back and forth to Sussex, announcing that he expected to 'have a man in about a fortnight'.

Months passed, however, as titbits of Jacks' successes appeared in the papers claiming that he had found new evidence and was following new leads. If nothing else, the continued interest in the murder from the family forced Scotland Yard to reopen the case. Jacks sent in his report and Joan's aunts applied for a very rare private prosecution. On 30 August 1950, much to everyone's surprise, especially the suspect's, the application was granted. Stillwell was arrested, remanded in custody, and the case was scheduled to be heard at Arundel Magistrates Court.

Arundel Castle close to the park where Joan was murdered
(iStock)

Despite the fact that everyone involved in tracking down evidence against Stillwell had absolute conviction that they had traced the right man, the fact was that a lot of time had now passed since Joan's murder. It became clear that over the past two years the key witnesses had become confused and forgetful. It was decided that the evidence against Stillwell was purely circumstantial and he had merely had the opportunity to commit the crime, with no hard evidence actually linking him to it. The case was now blocked from going to full trial.

Mr Jacks returned to his office in Bridlington. Soon he was to be in the newspapers again, but this time it was for receiving a fine of £2 for punching a 74-year-old bailiff at his office on the Promenade. However, there was to be no justice for Joan Woodhouse and the case remains unsolved.

THE BEXHILL TRAIN CRIME

FLORENCE NIGHTINGALE SHORE WAS A RELATIVE AND GOD-DAUGHTER OF THE NURSING PIONEER FLORENCE NIGHTINGALE. SHE HAD BEEN BORN INTO A WEALTHY FAMILY IN STAMFORD, LINCOLNSHIRE AND, LIKE HER FAMOUS RELATIVE, SHE HAD BECOME AN ARMY NURSE. FLORENCE HAD SERVED IN SOUTH AFRICA IN THE SECOND BOER WAR AND IN FRANCE DURING THE GREAT WAR. SHE HAD ONLY RECENTLY RETURNED FROM THE WESTERN FRONT AND HAD BEEN LIVING AT A NURSES' HOME IN HAMMERSMITH. TWO DAYS AFTER CELEBRATING HER 55TH BIRTHDAY ON 10 JANUARY 1920, SHE WAS CLUBBED TO DEATH ON THE LONDON TO HASTINGS TRAIN.

Although she was discovered at Bexhill Station, Florence had been attacked somewhere between Victoria and Polegate Junction and possibly even on the same stretch of track as Mr Gold had been attacked by Percy Mapleton (described elsewhere in this book). Florence had been particularly unfortunate to be on the train as it emerged that just the previous day she had been in Kent and she might easily have continued directly on

Bexhill, Railway Station

Bexhill station seen from Sea Road at about the time of the unsolved murder
(Courtesy of Bexhill Old Town Preservation Society)

to nearby St Leonards, to meet up with friends, rather than returning to London to set out afresh the following afternoon.

The train carrying Florence divided at Polegate Junction. It was there that three railway workers discovered the badly injured nurse in the corner of the carriage. Florence was still seated upright and they initially thought that she was sleeping, but on closer inspection the blood on her head revealed that she had been mortally injured. While there was no sign of a struggle, Florence was now without her money and her ticket. In addition to this her jewellery, including her diamond rings and an amethyst pendant, were also missing.

The railway workers at Bexhill took the decision to leave the badly injured nurse on board and allow the train to travel the short distance on to Hastings where the hospital was known to be close to the station. Florence was duly transferred to the hospital, where she stayed for the next four days. The medical staff fought to save her life, but she remained in a coma until she died on 16 January.

Now the full facts of Florence's life emerged. She had served with distinction in South Africa and then at the outbreak of the Great War, despite being 49 years of age, had rejoined the Queen's Nurses and been sent to work under the French Red Cross as a staff nurse and acting sister. She was seen in some of the newspapers as something of a heroine, and the police redoubled their efforts.

A nationwide hunt for Florence's killer was launched both in Sussex and in London as there was a belief that the murderer may well have instantly returned to the capital. A mystery train passenger in a brown suit, who left the nurse's carriage at the stop before Bexhill, was named by the police as the prime suspect. He had been seen in Nurse Shore's carriage standing at the window as the train had departed from London. Later a signalman near Wivelsfield said that he saw a partially opened door on the train, as if someone may have been contemplating jumping.

A suspect in some quarters was Percy Toplis, known as 'the monocled mutineer', but although these events were unfolding at the same time as Toplis was being hunted for his own crimes, there is no real possibility that he was involved in the death of Nurse Shore.

As the months passed the leads in the case became fewer and fewer. Soon the police were clutching at straws. In November there was a flurry of excitement as a hospital patient in Southampton, a music-hall artiste, confessed to the murder. But this 'remarkable development' in the case (as the newspapers called it) proved not to be all that remarkable, as the confession had not the slightest basis in reality.

There was a genuine sadness and disgust that a woman who had travelled so widely and served so bravely at various battlefronts was to meet her own death so pointlessly on a train in Sussex. To this day no one has ever been convicted of the brutal murder of Florence Nightingale Shore.

THE EASTBOURNE POLICE MURDER

AT ABOUT 7.15PM ON 9 OCTOBER 1912, A WOMAN WAS LEAVING A HOUSE IN EASTBOURNE TO HAVE DINNER AT A HOTEL IN THE GRAND PARADE. A COACHMAN, A MAN CALLED DAVID POTTER, WAS HIRED TO TAKE HER TO THE RESTAURANT. POTTER NOTICED A MAN APPARENTLY HIDING ON THE ROOF OF THE PORCH ABOVE THE FRONT DOOR. ONCE ROUND THE CORNER HE EXPLAINED THE SITUATION TO HIS PASSENGER. THE COACH RETURNED IMMEDIATELY AND THE WOMAN RE-ENTERED THE HOUSE ON THE PRETEXT OF HAVING FORGOTTEN SOMETHING. ONCE INSIDE SHE CALLED THE POLICE.

The woman making the call to the police was Countess Flora Sztaray. She was married to Wilhelm Stanek, who was the consul for the Austro-Hungarian Empire in Bulgaria, and had owned a house in Eastbourne for many years. With her title and her exotic background it was natural that she might be the target for burglars.

Inspector Walls arrived at the house about twenty minutes after the call was made. He shouted out in the dark to where the man was thought to be hiding. But rather than give himself up the intruder now fired a shot, fatally wounding the policeman. By chance the Chief Constable lived nearby and was soon on the scene, albeit that the murderer had by now escaped into the night.

Local residents were questioned and before long a witness came forward volunteering the identity of the murderer. The witness was a Dr Edgar Power of Finsbury Park and he promptly named the murderer as John Williams. Power refused to make a formal statement but said that he had further information, demanding absolute discretion and that his name be kept out of the investigation. For all of his suspicious behaviour much of Power's evidence did seem compelling.

Two days after his initial contact Power resurfaced and telephoned the Chief Inspector, stating that he was meeting with the suspect, John Williams, at Moorgate Street Station. It was here that Williams was arrested on suspicion of murder.

Florence Seymour, Williams's girlfriend, was also brought in for questioning. Florence denied knowing anything about the crime, but she was in possession of a cloakroom ticket for the left luggage office at Victoria Station, which attracted police interest. The associated bag was retrieved and while it did not contain the murder weapon, it did contain a revolver holster. There were also pawn tickets relating to stolen items taken from earlier crimes committed by Williams.

South Cliff Avenue, the street where the shooting took place
(By Oast House Archive)

With Williams remanded in custody, the mysterious Dr Power reappeared. His latest announcement was that he had knowledge of the murder weapon, which he claimed had been buried somewhere on the beach. Florence Seymour was questioned once again and eventually admitted her part in the affair and confirmed Power's story that the gun was hidden on the beach. With Florence's more precise directions the gun was retrieved and a forensic examination confirmed it was the one that had killed Inspector Walls.

The trial of John Williams began on 12 December 1912 at Lewes Assizes. Williams maintained that he was innocent of both murder and burglary, saying that the robbery was surely to do with the fact that the house-owner was the wife of a consul. Perhaps the burglary was an attempt to obtain papers for political purposes, which would not be his kind of crime at all. In some ways it was a reasonable defence as it was a time of intense diplomatic activity in the Balkans. The first Balkan war, pitching Bulgaria against the Ottoman Empire, was just days away.

Florence Seymour was the first person called to the witness box. She now said that her earlier statements implicating Williams were false, and that she had only said this because Edgar Power had told her that she would be charged with murder if she did not. This was at odds with Power's own testimony that Williams had shot the policeman and then openly bragged about it.

Williams asserted that the gun retrieved from the beach

was not his and had been given to him by a fellow thief called 'Freddy Mike', who had asked him to keep the package until Mike came to collect it. The explanation was not terribly plausible and after only fifteen minutes of deliberations the jury returned a verdict of guilty.

The beach, with the Redoubt in the background, where the murder weapon was hidden (The Author)

There have been question marks over Edgar Power's part in the tracing of Williams. His behaviour throughout has been seen as somewhat underhand, particularly so in arranging the operation at Moorgate to ensnare a friend. Indeed it seems that Power was not in fact a qualified doctor and that he was using an alias. However, it was to prove nothing compared to the list of false names used by Williams over the years.

Behind the set of aliases John Williams was really George Mackay, who was a former member of the Royal Scots regiment. Mackay had served in the Boer War and had been based in Kimberley in South Africa, which was famous at the time for its diamond mining. Perhaps this was where he got his taste for the expensive jewellery that he liked to steal. Eventually he had got into trouble for his thieving and was deported back to Britain to continue his life of crime.

There was to be an appeal, and 'Freddy Mike' actually turned up, at least in the form of a letter, but his highly implausible explanation which involved him having a twin brother was quickly discounted. George Mackay was executed at Lewes Gaol on 30 January 1913.